NICOLAS BRASCH

For Valour
Australia's Victoria Cross Heroes

This book is dedicated to the ninety-nine Australian VC recipients whose stories I have had the pleasure of researching and writing. They are the ninety-nine most inspiring and humbling stories I have ever come across. NB

First published in 2013
by black dog books
an imprint of Walker Books Australia Pty Ltd
Locked Bag 22, Newtown
NSW 2042 Australia
www.walkerbooks.com.au

National Library of Australia Cataloguing-in-Publication entry:
Brasch, Nicolas, 1961-
For valour: Australia's Victoria Cross heroes / Nicolas Brasch.
ISBN: 978 1 742032 31 3 (pbk.)
Series: Our stories.
Subjects: Victoria Cross.
Military decorations – Australia.
Australia – Armed Forces – Biography.
355.13420994

Typeset in Bembo
Printed and bound in China

10 9 8 7 6 5 4 3 2

IMAGE CREDITS Front cover: Army camp, Gallipoli, TP Bennett, State Library of Victoria; Mark Donaldson, Australian Department of Defence; Arthur Sullivan, A02497A, AWM; Hughie Edwards, 042687A, AWM; Neville Howse, A02711, AWM. Back cover: Hughie Edwards with Prime Minister John Curtin, UK1303, AWM; Albert Jacka, detail from Enlist in the Sportsmen's Thousand Poster, State Library of Victoria; William Dunstan, RC00758, Alexander Burton, RC09114, AWM. P1: Albert Jacka, detail from Enlist in the Sportsmen's Thousand Poster, State Library of Victoria. P2: Map of the ANZAC position, Gallipoli, State Library of Victoria. P3: Army camp, Gallipoli, TP Bennett, State Library of Victoria. P5: VC medal, RELAWM16499.001, AWM. P6: Neville Howse, A02711, AWM. P7: Australian troops in the South African War, 1899-1902, State Library of Victoria. P8/9: Equipment and supplies loaded on beach, Gallipoli, TP Bennett, State Library of Victoria. P10: Captain Albert Jacka, E00631, AWM; Enlist in the Sportsmen's Thousand, State Library of Victoria, and Enlist in the Sportsmen's Thousand Poster, State Library of Victoria. P11: Leonard Keysor, A04013, AWM. P12: Alexander Burton, RC09114, AWM; William Dunstan, RC00758, AWM; Frederick Tubb, P02939.004, AWM. P13: Hugo Throssell, P02939.005, AWM. P14: Percy Cherry, P02939.012, AWM. P15: Stanley McDougall, A05155, AWM. P14/15: Australian military cemetery, TP Bennett State Library of Victoria. P16: Phillip Davey, H19440, AWM. P17: Maurice Buckley, A03072A, AWM. P18: Reginald Inwood, H06193, AWM. P19: Frank McNamara, DAAV00004, AWM; Palestine, State Library of Victoria. P21: Arthur Sullivan, A02497A, AWM. P23 Troops in New Guinea, H92.57/29, State Library of Victoria. P24: Roden Cutler, 012576, AWM. P25: Hughie Edwards, 042687A, AWM; UK1303, AWM. P26: Bruce Kingsbury, P01637.001, AWM. P27: Richard Kelliher, 044652, AWM. P29 Keith Payne, LES/69/0594/VN, AWM; Peter Badcoe, P00942.002, AWM. P30: Benjamin Roberts-Smith, Australian Department of Defence. P31: Mark Donaldson, Australian Department of Defence.

THANKS
The author and publisher thank The Australian Defence Force for their assistance and expertise in the creation of this book.

Map of the
ANZAC POSITION
GALLIPOLI
illustrate Sir Ian Hamilton's despatch of December 11th, 1915.
1:20,000

Contents

Introducing the Victoria Cross (VC)

There is no greater military honour for Australian military personnel than to receive the Victoria Cross medal. The Victoria Cross (VC) is only ever awarded in times of war to people who risk their own lives to save others – the most heroic act imaginable. This is why the Victoria Cross is held in such high esteem.

Origins of the Victoria Cross

The Victoria Cross was first introduced in 1856 by Queen Victoria, which is how it got its name. It was initially introduced to honour British soldiers who had performed acts of heroism in the Crimean War. The Crimean War was fought from 1854 to 1856, between Britain, France and Turkey on one side, and Russia on the other side. The Victoria Cross can now be awarded to military personnel from Britain or any of the Commonwealth countries.

What's in a name?

In 1991, the name of the medal awarded to Australian military personnel was changed from the Victoria Cross to the Victoria Cross for Australia. However, its design remains the same.

What the VC is made from

The Victoria Cross has two parts to it: a bronze Maltese cross and a crimson ribbon. The cross is not made from just any bronze. It is bronze taken from Russian cannons that were captured by the British during the Crimean War.

Posthumous recipients

Posthumous means after death. Of the ninety-nine Australians who have received the Victoria Cross, twenty-six were awarded the medal posthumously. Several of the others died in battles after they had received the VC.

For Valour

"For Valour". These are the only words that appear on the Victoria Cross medal. These two simple words, meaning "for an act of courage or bravery", neatly sum up the reasons why a Victoria Cross is awarded.

Rank

Australian VC recipients come from all ranks in the military. To date there are no VC recipients from the Royal Australian Navy. Here is a guide to selected ranks in the army and air force in order of highest to lowest.

Royal Australian Army

Field Marshal
General
Lieutenant General
Major General
Brigadier
Colonel
Lieutenant Colonel
Major
Captain
Lieutenant
Second Lieutenant
Warrant Officer
Staff Sergeant
Sergeant
Lance Sergeant
Bombardier
Corporal
Lance Bombardier
Lance Corporal
Trooper
Signaller
Sapper
Gunner
Private

Royal Australian Air Force

Marshal of the RAAF
Air Chief Marshal
Air Marshal
Air Vice Marshal
Air Commodore
Group Captain
Wing-Commander
Squadron Leader
Flight Lieutenant
Flying Officer
Pilot Officer
Warrant Officer
Flight Sergeant
Sergeant
Corporal
Leading Aircraftman/woman
Aircraftman/woman

Crimson ribbon
Laurel leaves
Crown of Saint Edward
FOR VALOUR

Boer War

The Boer War took place in South Africa from 1899–1902. It was fought between British and Commonwealth forces on one side, and the Boers (Dutch South Africans) on the other.

Why the war was fought

During the 1600s and 1700s, the Dutch and the British colonised (took over) parts of southern Africa. The discovery of gold and diamonds in the late 1800s saw the British and Boers fight over the land. In 1899, a full-scale war broke out.

Why Australians became involved

As a part of the Commonwealth, Australians felt bound to support Britain. There was no federal government in Australia when the war began, so at first the colonies (now states) sent troops to South Africa to fight with the British. After Federation, in 1901, when the colonies joined to become one nation, troops were sent to represent Australia.

Full name: Neville Reginald Howse
Born: 26 October 1863, Somerset, England
Died: 19 September 1930, London, England
Rank at time of action: Captain
Unit: NSW Army Medical Corps

Neville Howse

Neville Howse was the first Australian to be awarded the VC. He is also the only Australian to have been awarded the VC while serving as a medical officer.

Doctor on horseback

Neville Howse was born in England. His father was a doctor and Howse also studied medicine before moving to Australia because his health could not cope with the cold British winters. While working as a doctor in New South Wales, he also became a keen horserider. When the Boer War broke out, he had no hesitation in signing up as a medical officer on horseback.

Saving a trumpeter

On 24 July 1900, Howse saw a trumpeter fall after being shot. Howse jumped onto a horse and raced towards the injured man to treat him. As he rode, Howse came under heavy fire and his horse was shot dead underneath him. Howse continued on foot and crawled on his stomach to evade gunfire, until he reached the injured trumpeter. He patched up the man's wounds, carried him to safety and operated on his bladder. The operation saved the trumpeter's life.

Gallipoli, knighthood and Parliament

During World War I, Howse served at Gallipoli and took a major role in evacuating wounded soldiers. He received a knighthood in 1917 and later became a member of Federal Parliament, serving as Minister for Defence and Minister for Health.

AUSTRALIAN VC RECIPIENTS

Six Australians were awarded VCs during the Boer War:

Frederick Bell
John Bisdee
Neville Howse
Leslie Maygar
James Rogers
Guy Wylly

World War I

World War I was fought from 1914–1918. On one side were Germany, Austria-Hungary and Italy, known as the Triple Alliance. On the other side were Britain, France and Russia, known as the Triple Entente. Several other nations fought as well, including Turkey, as part of the Triple Alliance; and Australia and the USA, as part of the Triple Entente.

Why the war started

Russia and Serbia had a longstanding agreement that Russia would help Serbia if it ever came under attack. So when the Austria-Hungary government declared war on Serbia after a Serbian assassinated the heir to the Austro-Hungarian throne, Russia declared war on Austria-Hungary.

Germany and Austria-Hungary had a similar agreement. So when Russia declared war on Austria-Hungary, Germany declared war on Russia.

France had an agreement with Russia, so it declared war on Germany.

Germany invaded Belgium because it stood between Germany and France. Germany wanted to get into France before the French had a chance to properly prepare themselves for war.

Britain had a longstanding agreement to help Belgium if Belgium was invaded. So Britain declared war on Germany.

And when Britain entered the conflict, so did the colonies that made up the British Commonwealth, including Australia and New Zealand.

The Western Front

The Western Front was the name given to the battlefields in France and Belgium. More than 50,000 Australian soldiers were killed on the Western Front.

Gallipoli

The Gallipoli Peninsula, on the coast of Turkey, was the scene of the first intense fighting for Australian troops in World War I. The Australians landed there on 25 April 1915 – we now commemorate ANZAC Day on that date. More than 8000 Australian soldiers were killed at Gallipoli.

Palestine

The fighting in Palestine, in the Middle East, was based around gaining control of the Suez Canal. Whichever side could control the Suez Canal would have the advantage of being able to transport soldiers by ship between Asia and Europe without going around Africa.

East Africa

No official Australian unit fought in East Africa (now Kenya) but Wilbur Dartnell from Melbourne was awarded a VC for his actions there while fighting for the British Army.

AUSTRALIAN VC RECIPIENTS

Sixty-four Australians were awarded VCs during World War I:

Thomas Axford
Robert Beatham
Frederick Birks
Arthur Blackburn
Albert Borella
Walter Brown
Alexander Buckley
Maurice Buckley
Patrick Bugden
Alexander Burton
John Carroll
George Cartwright
Claud Castleton
Percy Cherry
Thomas Cooke
William Currey
Henry Dalziel
Wilbur Dartnell
Phillip Davey
William Dunstan
John Dwyer
Alfred Gaby
Bernard Gordon
Robert Grieve
Arthur Hall
John Hamilton
George Howell
George Ingram
Reginald Inwood
Albert Jacka
William Jackson
Clarence Jeffries
Jørgen Jensen
William Joynt
Bede Kenny
Leonard Keysor
John Leak
Albert Lowerson
Lawrence McCarthy
Stanley McDougall
Lewis McGee
Frank McNamara
Robert Mactier
Joseph Maxwell
Rupert Moon
Henry Murray
James Newland
Martin O'Meara
Walter Peeler
Charles Pope
William Ruthven
John Ryan
Clifford Sadlier
Alfred Shout
Percy Statton
Percy Storkey
William Symons
Hugo Throssell
Edgar Towner
Frederick Tubb
Blair Wark
Lawrence Weathers
John Whittle
James Woods

Albert Jacka

Albert Jacka left Australian shores in 1914 as an unknown private, keen for adventure. He returned a hero, described by the official war historian, Charles Bean, as "the symbol of the spirit of the ANZACs".

In the trenches

Jacka was the first Australian to receive a VC for his actions at Gallipoli. On 19 May 1915, some Turkish soldiers attacked and captured an Australian trench. This brought them close to other Australian soldiers. Jacka jumped into the trench full of Turkish soldiers. He shot five of them and bayoneted two more. The rest of the soldiers in the trench fled. When a senior officer arrived, Jacka told him, "I managed to get the beggars, sir!"

Full name: Albert Jacka
Born: 10 January 1893, Layard, Victoria
Died: 17 January 1932, Melbourne, Victoria
Rank at time of action: Lance Corporal
Unit: 14th Battalion

Three times a hero

Albert Jacka received two other medals for courage during WWI, both in France. In 1916 he was awarded the Military Cross after leading a small group of men in an attack against a much larger group of Germans who had taken some Australian soldiers prisoner. Jacka was shot several times but still managed to free his comrades and capture the Germans. He also received a bar for his Military Cross for another heroic deed.

When Albert Jacka died at just 39 years of age, more than 6000 people filed by his coffin to get one last glimpse of this amazing war hero. His early death was believed to be a result of war wounds and depression from a failing business.

A poster featuring Albert Jacka, encouraging men to enlist. "No more fearless or gallant soldier took part in the Great War," said Newton Wanliss, military historian.

Leonard Keysor

Leonard Keysor was a bomb thrower. The actions for which he received his VC were so incredible that he was asked to re-enact them years later for a movie. Keysor was one of seven Australians to be awarded VCs for their actions at Lone Pine during the Gallipoli campaign.

Howzat!

A bomb thrower's job usually involved lighting and throwing small bombs towards the enemy, and smothering enemy bombs with sandbags or clothing before they could explode. But on 7–8 August 1915, Keysor took his bomb throwing duties to the extreme. As Turkish bombs landed near him and his colleagues, he picked them up before they exploded and threw them back at the Turks. After a while he became even more confident and started catching Turkish bombs in midair, much like a fielder in cricket, and hurling them straight back.

Re-enactment

When Keysor was asked to re-enact his bomb throwing exploits for a film, one of the "prop" bombs exploded and he required hospital treatment.

Full name: Leonard Maurice Keysor
Born: 3 November 1885, London, England
Died: 12 October 1951, London, England
Rank at time of action: Lance Corporal
Unit: 1st Battalion

The Lone Pine trenches after a bombing. Leonard Keysor is centre rear, wearing a slouch hat and looking at the camera. "[Going to war] was the only adventure I ever had." Leonard Keysor.

Alexander Burton, William Dunstan and Frederick Tubb

Alexander Burton, William Dunstan and Frederick Tubb are the only Australians to have received VCs fighting alongside each other. Burton was the first Australian to be awarded a VC posthumously.

Full name: Frederick Harold Tubb
Born: 28 November 1881, Longwood, Victoria
Died: 20 September 1917, Ypres, Belgium
Rank at time of action: Lieutenant
Unit: 7th Battalion

Defending the trench

On 9 August 1915, at Gallipoli, Alexander Burton, William Dunstan and Frederick Tubb were among ten men defending a trench from fierce Turkish attack. This trench led to a network of other trenches and if it had been captured, many Australian soldiers would have been killed. The Turkish attacks killed or seriously wounded seven of the men, leaving just Burton, Dunstan and Tubb to withstand bombs, bullets and bayonets. They defended the trench so well that the much larger number of Turks eventually gave up – though by that stage Burton had been killed.

Full name: Alexander Stewart Burton
Born: 20 January 1893, Kyneton, Victoria
Died: 9 August 1915, Gallipoli, Turkey
Rank at time of action: Corporal
Unit: 7th Battalion

Full name: William Dunstan
Born: 8 March 1895, Ballarat, Victoria
Died: 2 March 1957, Melbourne, Victoria
Rank at time of action: Corporal
Unit: 7th Battalion

Hugo Throssell

Hugo Throssell may have gone to war full of enthusiasm and returned a hero, but after the death of his brother in the war, Throssell became an anti-war campaigner.

Tennis over the traverse

Throssell was awarded his VC for defending a place called Hill 60 at Gallipoli on 29–30 August 1915. During this period, more than 3000 bombs were thrown back and forth, prompting the scene to be described as "a kind of tennis over the traverse and sandbags." Throssell was badly wounded but "refused to leave his post or to obtain medical assistance till all danger was passed". Even after being treated for facial wounds, he returned to the scene and continued to lead his men in battle.

Light Horse

Hugo Throssell is the only Australian to have received a VC as a member of a Light Horse regiment. Soldiers in these regiments were trained to fight while on horseback, though they often fought on the ground, as Throssell did in the campaign for which he was awarded his VC.

Famous family

Hugo Throssell's father was the second premier of Western Australia. Throssell's wife was Katharine Susannah Prichard, a famous novelist.

Full name: Hugo Vivian Hope Throssell
Born: 26 October 1884, Northam, West Australia
Died: 19 November 1933, Greenmount, West Australia
Rank at time of action: Second Lieutenant
Unit: 10th Light Horse Regiment, New Zealand and Australian Division

Percy Cherry

Percy Cherry was once involved in a gun battle with a German officer. At one point they both fired at the same time, hitting each other. Cherry was injured, but not as badly as the German. Cherry approached the man, who was clearly dying. The German soldier handed Cherry a package of letters and made him promise to post them to the German's family. When Cherry agreed, the soldier muttered, "And so it ends", and then died.

Capture the village

Cherry was awarded his VC posthumously. On 26 March 1917, he helped lead a campaign to capture the village of Lagnicourt in France, which had been taken by the Germans. During the campaign, all the other officers were killed or wounded, leaving Cherry in charge. Even after being shot in the leg, he refused to leave his post, and captured the village. However, he was eventually killed by an enemy bullet.

Full name: Percy Herbert Cherry
Born: 4 June 1895, Drysdale, Victoria
Died: 26 March 1917, Lagnicourt, France
Rank at time of action: Captain
Unit: 26th Battalion

Stanley McDougall

Stanley McDougall was involved in two amazing acts of bravery, in the same place, within eight days of each other. For the first he was awarded the VC; for the second the Military Medal. But that wasn't the end of his heroic acts. After the war, he worked for the Tasmanian Forestry Department and again became a hero rescuing people from bushfires.

Single-handed

On 28 March 1918, McDougall was on lookout duty at Dernancourt, France, when he noticed German troops advancing. He called for help but the unit that came to their aid was hit by a bomb. McDougall then grabbed the Lewis machine gun that the unit had with them and ran at the Germans, firing as he went. He killed and wounded several of them but then noticed other German troops approaching. He was now single-handedly attacking more than thirty enemy soldiers. He kept firing until he ran out of ammunition. At that point he grabbed a bayonet, charged at a group of Germans, wounded them, then grabbed another gun. The Germans then surrendered in fear.

Full name: Stanley Robert McDougall
Born: 23 July 1889, Recherche, Tasmania
Died: 7 July 1968, Scottsdale, Tasmania
Rank at time of action: Sergeant
Unit: 47th Battalion

Phillip Davey

Phillip Davey was not the only member of his family to receive an award for bravery during World War I. His brothers, Claude and Richard, were both awarded the Military Medal. Phillip was also awarded the Military Medal for rescuing a wounded colleague while under heavy enemy fire.

Taking charge

Davey was part of a platoon that came under heavy German fire on 28 June 1918, at Merris, France. When the commander of his unit was killed, the unit was forced to take shelter and Davey took matters into his own hands. He ran towards the attacking Germans and lobbed grenades at them. When he ran out of grenades, he returned to get more, then continued his attack until he had killed all the enemy soldiers. He then took their machine gun and used it on another advancing party of Germans until they retreated.

Full name: Phillip Davey
Born: 10 October 1896, Unley, South Australia
Died: 21 December 1953, Adelaide, South Australia
Rank at time of action: Corporal
Unit: 10th Battalion

Maurice Buckley

Maurice Buckley signed up for the army in 1914, soon after the war began. However, he was discharged after deserting. He signed up again in 1916 under a false name, Gerald Sexton. "Gerald" was the first name of his dead brother while "Sexton" was his mother's maiden name. It was under the name Gerald Sexton that he was awarded the VC.

Prisoners galore

On 18 September 1918, near Le Verguier in France, Buckley was involved in several actions that severely weakened the German hold on the area. First, he rushed and captured a German machine-gun post. Next he put a German trench out of action. Buckley then fired into a German dugout and captured thirty Germans. By the end of the day, he had attacked several other dugouts and taken nearly 100 German soldiers as prisoners.

An unfortunate accident

Buckley may have survived several near misses during battle, but he died just three years after the war from an injury sustained falling off a horse. At his funeral his coffin was carried by ten fellow Victoria Cross recipients.

Full name: Maurice Vincent Buckley
Born: 13 April 1891, Melbourne, Victoria
Died: 27 January 1921, Melbourne, Victoria
Rank at time of action: Sergeant
Unit: 13th Battalion

Reginald Inwood

Reginald Inwood was living in Broken Hill when he enlisted in the army. Many people in that town were opposed to the war and made their feelings known. When Inwood returned from the war as a hero, he reminded people that he had been stoned at the station when he left, but "those mongrels were the first to ... shake me by the hand" when he returned.

One ... two ... three acts of bravery

Reginald Inwood was awarded his VC for three separate acts of bravery over 20–21 September 1917, at Polygon Wood, Belgium. First, Inwood went ahead of his colleagues and took an enemy position, killing several Germans and capturing several more. Then he snuck into enemy territory to observe operations and report his findings back to his commanders. Finally, along with a fellow soldier, he crept up behind a German machine-gun post that was firing on the Australians and killed all but one of the enemy soldiers operating it.

Full name: Reginald Roy Inwood
Born: 14 July 1890, Adelaide, South Australia
Died: 23 October 1971, Adelaide, South Australia
Rank at time of action: Private
Unit: 10th Battalion

Frank McNamara

Frank McNamara was the first Australian airman to be awarded the VC. He was also the only Australian to receive the VC for actions in the Palestine campaign.

Flying into danger

On 20 March 1917, McNamara was one of several British and Australian pilots flying missions over Palestine. Several planes were hit by ground fire, including McNamara's. One of the bullets hit his leg and he turned his plane around to seek medical treatment. Suddenly, he noticed that another pilot had been hit by gunfire and forced to land. McNamara could see Turkish soldiers advancing towards the downed plane. He landed his own aircraft near the damaged one, and rescued the other pilot. As they attempted to take off, McNamara's plane became damaged. They rushed back to the other pilot's plane and worked on fixing the engine and propeller, all the while shooting at the approaching Turks. Finally, they got the plane working and took off.

But that wasn't the end of their troubles. McNamara was losing blood fast. Several times he had to stick his head out of the window, into the icy wind, to stop himself losing consciousness. He managed to land the plane safely – then collapsed. He was rushed to hospital and at one point was pronounced dead. But he survived, and went on to teach other military pilots, many of whom flew during World War II.

Full name: Francis Hubert McNamara
Born: 4 April 1894, Rushworth, Victoria
Died: 2 November 1961, Amersham, England
Rank at time of action: Lieutenant
Unit: No. 1 Squadron, Australian Flying Corps

North Russia Campaign

The North Russia Campaign started almost immediately after the end of World War I. Russia had withdrawn from World War I in 1917, as it faced its own civil unrest.

Why the war was fought

In October 1917, a group of Russians known as the Bolsheviks took over control of Russia. They wanted to create a new system of government known as communism – a system they believed was fairer for the working people of Russia. The British government was concerned that weapons provided to the former Russian government might be used to fight the British. They also believed that a communist government in Russia posed a threat to peace in Europe. So the British sent some troops to try and help the former government regain control – but they failed.

Why Australians became involved

There was no official Australian military unit sent to North Russia. However, about 150 Australians signed up to fight with the British forces that numbered 8000. Nine of the Australians had fought at Gallipoli and the Western Front but were obviously not worn out by war. Some Australians may have signed up because there was little work for them back home. Some had to gain permission from the Australian military before being accepted, because they had not been officially discharged. The Australian officials only gave permission for unmarried men to take part.

AUSTRALIAN VC RECIPIENTS

Only five men received VCs during the North Russia Campaign – and two of them were Australians:

Samuel Pearse
Arthur Sullivan

Arthur Sullivan

Arthur Sullivan enlisted to fight in World War I in April 1918. However, the war was over before he could face the enemy. Still keen to see some military action, he volunteered to fight in North Russia.

Saved from drowning

On 10 August 1919, Sullivan's unit was walking over a narrow bridge when it came under heavy enemy fire. The bridge collapsed and four men fell into the swamp below. Sullivan dived in and rescued them one at a time, despite being fired on constantly. His VC citation read in part: "But for this gallant action his comrades would undoubtedly have drowned".

Samuel Pearse

was another recipient of the Victoria Cross during the North Russia Campaign. Citations were given along with the soldiers' VCs. Samuel Pearse's read: "Sergeant Pearse cut his way through enemy barbed wire under very heavy machine-gun and rifle fire and cleared a way for the troops to enter an enemy battery position. Seeing that a blockhouse was harassing our advance and causing us casualties, he charged the blockhouse single-handed, killing the occupants with bombs. This gallant non-commissioned officer met with his death a minute later, and it was due to him that the position was carried with so few casualties. His magnificent bravery and utter disregard for personal danger won for him the admiration of all troops."

Full name: Arthur Percy Sullivan
Born: 27 November 1896, Prospect, South Australia
Died: 9 April 1937, London, England
Rank at time of action: Corporal
Unit: 45th Battalion, Royal Fusiliers

World War II

World War II was fought from 1939–1945. On one side were the countries known as the Axis powers, including Germany, Italy and Japan. On the other side were the countries known as the Allies, including Britain, the Soviet Union, the USA, Australia, Canada and New Zealand. The war was fought in Europe, Africa, the Middle East and the Pacific.

Why the war was fought

The causes of World War II can be traced back to the end of World War I. After Germany had been defeated, it was ordered to pay a great deal of compensation to the countries they had been fighting. As a result the German people suffered great economic hardship. This caused resentment among the Germans. One man was able to tap into this resentment and restore German pride. His name was Adolf Hitler. Through a combination of fear and force, he managed to take control of Germany. He then started murdering opponents and invading neighbouring countries. On 3 September 1939, Britain declared war on Germany.

Why Australians became involved

The Australian Prime Minister in 1939 was Robert Menzies. He believed that if Britain was under attack, then Australia should automatically help. He declared war on Germany the same day as Britain did. When Japan entered the war, Australia came under direct attack, and Australian troops were recalled from Europe to defend the Pacific.

Tobruk

Tobruk, Libya, is in the Middle East. This was an important location during World War II, because whoever controlled it was able to easily move their troops in and out of other parts of the Middle East. Between April and August 1941, more than 3000 Australians were killed or wounded while preventing the Germans taking Tobruk.

Bombing of Darwin

On 19 February 1942, the Northern Australian city of Darwin was bombed by Japanese planes. The raid killed 252 people. But it was not the only time Darwin was bombed. Over the next eighteen months, the Japanese bombed Darwin a further sixty-three times.

Kokoda

The Kokoda Trail in Papua was the scene of fierce fighting between Australian and Japanese troops during the second half of 1942. The fighting claimed more than 600 Australian lives while more than 13,000 Japanese died in Papua.

AUSTRALIAN VC RECIPIENTS
Twenty Australians received VCs during World War II:

Charles Anderson
Albert Chowne
Roden Cutler
Thomas Derrick
John Edmondson
Hughie Edwards
John French
James Gordon
Percival Gratwick
Stan Gurney
Richard Kelliher
Edward Kenna
William Kibby
Bruce Kingsbury
John Mackey
Rawdon Middleton
William Newton
Frank Partridge
Reginald Rattey
Leslie Starcevich

Roden Cutler

Roden Cutler's war service was only the start of a distinguished career in public service. After the war he served as Australian High Commissioner in New Zealand (1946–52), Ceylon (now Sri Lanka) (1952–55), Pakistan, (1958–61); Australian delegate to the United Nations General Assembly (1962–64) and Governor of New South Wales (1966–81).

Communications

Cutler was awarded his VC for several actions over eighteen days of fighting in Lebanon. First, he fixed a broken telephone line while under enemy machine-gun fire. He then used machine guns to drive back several German tanks. On another occasion, he set up observation posts along a road under enemy control. These posts were pivotal in attacking the enemy. Finally, he was laying a telephone line so that units could communicate with each other when one of his legs was shot to pieces. Two enemy soldiers appeared above him, guns in hand. Instead of finishing him off, they left him to die in his own time. He survived, but his leg had to be amputated.

Full name: Arthur Roden Cutler
Born: 24 May 1916, Sydney, New South Wales
Died: 21 February 2002, Sydney, New South Wales
Rank at time of action: Lieutenant
Unit: 2/5th Field Regiment

Roden Cutler with the Governor General, Lord Gowrie, at Admiralty House after receiving his Victoria Cross.

Hughie Edwards

Hughie Edwards was almost killed while bailing from a damaged plane in 1938, but survived to become a war hero just four years later. Edwards was flying with the British Royal Air Force (RAF), rather than the Royal Australian Air Force (RAAF), when he was awarded his VC. He was one of only two Australian pilots who received the VC for action over Europe during World War II. Later in life he served as Governor of Western Australia.

Fly and run

On 4 July 1941, Edwards led fifteen aircraft on a bombing raid over the German town of Bremen. It had to be done in broad daylight, meaning they would be spotted and fired upon by German ships and ground forces. To make certain his bombs hit their target, Edwards flew as low as he could, so low that he flew underneath telegraph lines. Despite his plane being hit by enemy fire at least twenty times, Edwards managed to drop his bombs and return to England.

Happy meal

Several weeks later, Edwards was dining in a restaurant when news came through that a pilot named Edwards had been awarded the VC. It was only when it was mentioned that the man was an Australian that Edwards realised it was him.

Hughie Edwards talking to Mr John Curtin, Prime Minister of Australia, during his visit to the RAF station.

Full name: Hughie Idwal Edwards
Born: 1 August 1914, Fremantle, West Australia
Died: 5 August 1982, Sydney, New South Wales
Rank at time of action: Acting Wing-Commander
Unit: No. 105 Squadron, RAF

Bruce Kingsbury

Bruce Kingsbury was the only person to be awarded the VC for action during the Kokoda campaign. He had fought in the Middle East before being shipped back to the Pacific to fight along the Kokoda Trail.

Clearing a path

On 29 August 1942, Japanese troops were close to capturing the headquarters of the Australian 2/14th Battalion. Urgent action was required but there were few commanders still alive to plan a strategy. This did not deter Kingsbury. He surged towards the enemy, firing as he went. He killed a number of Japanese soldiers and cleared a path, which other Australian troops used to defend the headquarters. Kingsbury was shot dead in the process but his actions saved the headquarters and many Australian lives.

Place name

The Melbourne suburb of Kingsbury is named after Bruce Kingsbury.

Full name: Bruce Steel Kingsbury
Born: 8 January 1918, Melbourne, Victoria
Died: 29 August 1942, Isurava, Papua
Rank at time of action: Private
Unit: 2/14th Battalion

Richard Kelliher

Richard Kelliher found trouble along the Kokoda Trail in Papua, and not just with the enemy. In November 1942, he was accused of running from his unit during action, and saying, "It's too bloody hot for me. I am not a bloody fool". He was originally found guilty of desertion, ending his army career. However, he won an appeal and was then sent to New Guinea to fight in 1943.

All three men in this photo are recipients of the Victoria Cross. Richard Kelliher is centre, on the left is Frank John Partridge, and on the right is Reginald Rattey.

Bringing him in

Kelliher was fighting in New Guinea when, on 13 September 1943, his unit came under heavy fire from the Japanese. Several of his colleagues were killed, while others were badly wounded, including his commander, Billy Richards. Kelliher apparently turned to a colleague and muttered, "I'd better bring him in". He then gathered some grenades and threw them at the enemy posts, grabbed a gun and ran into the open, firing as he went. Despite being shot at the whole time, he dragged Richards to safety. "I wanted to bring Billy back because he was my cobber," Kelliher said later.

Full name: Richard Kelliher
Born: 1 September 1910, Ballybranagh, Ireland
Died: 28 January 1963, Melbourne, Victoria
Rank at time of action: Private
Unit: 2/25th Battalion

Vietnam War

The Vietnam War was fought from the late 1950s to 1975. Participation in the Vietnam War divided many countries, with large anti-war protests taking place in Australia during the 1960s.

Why the war was fought

Throughout much of its history, Vietnam has been colonised by other countries. In 1945, Vietnamese nationalists led by Ho Chi Minh rose up against the French, who controlled the country at that time. In 1954, Vietnam was divided into two: North Vietnam controlled by Ho Chi Minh under a system of communism; and South Vietnam which remained fiercely anti-communist. However, Ho Chi Minh wanted to control the whole country and began military action against the south. The United States government did not want the system of communism to expand, and sent in troops to protect South Vietnam. By 1975, the war was over and the communists controlled the whole country.

Why Australians became involved

The Australian government supported the actions of the United States government and felt obliged to provide some troops. In total about 50,000 Australians were sent to Vietnam, many of who were conscripted (forced to go). More than 500 Australians were killed.

AUSTRALIAN VC RECIPIENTS
Four Australians received Victoria Cross medals during the Vietnam War:

Peter Badcoe
Keith Payne
Ray Simpson
Kevin Wheatley

Peter Badcoe and Keith Payne

Peter Badcoe and Keith Payne were both sent to Vietnam as part of the Australian Army Training Team Vietnam to help train and advise the South Vietnamese troops.

Keith Payne (far right) is congratulated by a fellow member of the Australian Army Training Team at the announcement that he is to receive the Victoria Cross.

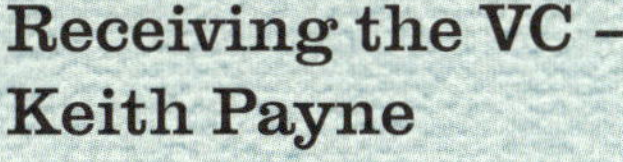

Receiving the VC – Keith Payne

On 24 May 1969, Payne was in charge of a group of South Vietnamese soldiers who came under heavy attack. Several were wounded, others fled in panic. After the rest had retreated to safety, Payne, who was injured, went searching for missing and stranded soldiers. Over the next few hours he found about forty of them, and helped them reach safety.

Full name: Keith Payne
Born: 30 August 1933, Ingham, Queensland
Rank at time of action: Warrant Officer Class II
Unit: Australian Army Training Team Vietnam

Full name: Peter John Badcoe
Born: 11 January 1934, Adelaide, South Australia
Died: 7 April 1967, Huong Tra District, South Vietnam
Rank at time of action: Major
Unit: Australian Army Training Team Vietnam

Receiving the VC – Peter Badcoe

Badcoe was awarded the VC for three separate actions over a six-week period. On 23 February 1967, he ran through enemy fire to rescue a wounded American medical adviser. On 7 March, he led a group of South Vietnamese who held off an enemy company that seemed certain to capture a key position. Finally, on 7 April, Badcoe stood in front of his company to throw a grenade at the enemy when he was shot and killed.

War in Afghanistan

The war in Afghanistan began in 2001, shortly after terrorist attacks on the United States by the al-Qaeda terrorist organisation. Many western countries committed troops to this war, including the USA, Great Britain, Germany, France and Australia. They are fighting a number of different groups, including the Taliban, who used to control Afghanistan.

Why the war is being fought

When al-Qaeda carried out terrorist attacks against the United States in 2001, the United States retaliated by attacking Iraq and Afghanistan. Their motivation was to capture the leader of al-Qaeda, Osama Bin Laden. However, they also declared that they wanted to end the Taliban's rule in Afghanistan, partly because the Taliban encouraged terrorism against the west; but also because the Taliban imprisoned and murdered Afghans who opposed its rule.

Why Australians became involved

The Australian government supported the actions of the United States government and sent troops to Afghanistan.

Receiving the VC – Benjamin Roberts-Smith

On 11 June 2010, Roberts-Smith deliberately engaged enemy forces to attract them away from some of his colleagues. He then attacked two enemy machine-gun posts and took them out of action. This enabled his patrol "to break into the enemy's defences and to regain the initiative ... resulting in a tactical victory" (official citation for Roberts-Smith's VC).

Full name: Benjamin Roberts-Smith
Born: 1 November 1978, Perth, Western Australia
Rank at time of action: Corporal
Unit: Special Air Service Regiment

Benjamin Roberts-Smith and Mark Donaldson

Mark Donaldson and Benjamin Roberts-Smith are both members of the elite Special Air Service Regiment (SAS) of the Australian Army.

Receiving the VC – Mark Donaldson

On 2 September 2008, Donaldson was travelling in a group made up of Australian, American and Afghan troops that was ambushed by the Taliban. Many soldiers were wounded. Donaldson deliberately moved into the open and started firing at the enemy, so that they would fire back at him. This enabled his wounded colleagues to be moved to cover. He also rescued a wounded Afghan interpreter who was lying in the open under heavy gunfire.

Full name: Mark Gregor Strang Donaldson
Born: 2 April 1979, Newcastle, New South Wales
Rank at time of action: Trooper
Unit: Special Air Service Regiment

AUSTRALIAN VC RECIPIENTS

Three Australians have been awarded VCs during the War in Afghanistan:

Mark Donaldson
Daniel Keighran
Benjamin Roberts-Smith

Glossary

ambush	a surprise attack
assassinate	when someone is intentionally killed, usually for political reasons
bar	the Military Cross can be received once only. For second and subsequent acts of bravery, a bar to add to the original medal is awarded
battalion	an army unit comprised of up to 1000 soldiers and support crew, usually led by a lieutenant colonel
blockhouse	a military structure, built from strong materials, from which soldiers can fire on or observe the enemy
Bolshevik	a communist from early 20th century Russia
campaign	the actions of an army during a specific period of time
casualties	people that are killed or wounded during war
citation	a record of action for a soldier or military unit
cobber	an Australian slang term for friend
colonised	a country being ruled by the government of another country
Commonwealth	a group of countries that share a common ruler (currently Queen Elizabeth II)
conscripted	when a person is forced into military service
desertion	when a person abandons military service, with no intention of returning
division	a large military unit made up of two or more regiments and can be between 10,000 and 30,000 soldiers, usually led by a major general
federation	the joining together of separate states under one central government
High Commissioner	the most important representative of a Commonwealth country living in another member country
interpreter	a person who translates one language into another
knighthood	a title given to people that achieve great things while serving their country
Military Cross	awarded to officers of the Commonwealth for "exemplary gallantry during active operations against the enemy" on land
non-commissioned	when an active soldier is chosen for a higher rank
platoon	a small group of soldiers, led by a lieutenant
posthumous	something that takes place after death
RAAF	the Royal Australian Air Force
RAF	the British Royal Air Force
regiment	an army unit made up of two or more battalions, usually led by a colonel
SAS	Special Air Service Regiment; an elite unit of the Australian army
squadron	an air force unit made up of two or more aircraft

Index